Living with Death

Journal Activities for Personal Growth

For Middle Grades

by

Judith Bisignano, O.P., Ed.D.

illustrated by **Darcy Tom**

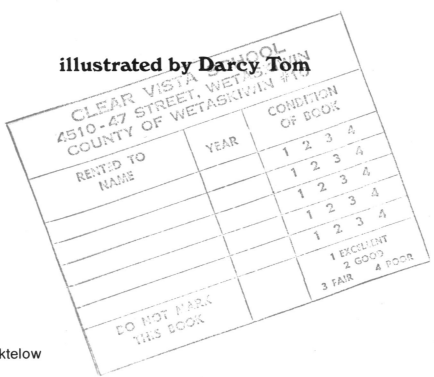

Cover by Paul Manktelow

Copyright © Good Apple, 1991

ISBN No. 0-86653-584-5

Printing No. 987654321

Good Apple
1204 Buchanan St., Box 299
Carthage, IL 62321-0299

Simon & Schuster Supplementary Education Group

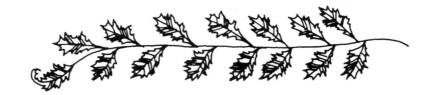

Author's Note

I have several reasons for writing this book. At the age of 22, I had a very negative experience in the death of my sister. Fifteen years later, I had a very positive death experience with the passage of my mother.

I want very much to assist children to have positive death experiences at a very young age. Children can share in the lives of dying relatives and friends. Children can join adults in the grieving process over the loss of a loved one.

As I write this book, I am in the process of dealing with my third bout with cancer. Each separate occurrence has been a mini death. At this time, I am *preparing to die*. I cannot experience my death until the time and moment of my transition to that new state of awareness. What I can experience is life. *Preparing to die*, then, is really *preparing to live.*

It is my sincerest hope that the activities in this book will assist teachers and parents to help children to participate appropriately in the death experiences of life and the life experiences of death.

Judy Bisignano, O.P., Ed.D.

In Memory Of

Danny Kinerk (May 17, 1962-September 5, 1980)
Leslie Bressert (January 27, 1963-August 25, 1981)
John Piel (March 6, 1969-September 19, 1981)
Michelle de Tiege (February 4, 1970-April 25, 1982)

Because of you, we emerge with a greater understanding of death and a greater commitment to life.

In Appreciation

There is no way to adequately show my appreciation to all those who offered significant suggestions towards the completion of this work. However, I sincerely thank Rose Audretsch, Nancy Bachelier, Lee Bergman, Walter and Teresa Bressert, Robert Calmes, Mary Jane Cera, Molly Cloud, Patti Crowley, Sue Fox, Michelle Fulton, Carol Habra, Julie Hayes, Libby Hilmar, Susan Huppe, Burt and Nancy Kinerk, Elisabeth Kubler-Ross, Mary Anne McElmurry, Lois Paha, Craig and Mary Ellen Piel, Joanne Pifer, Clorinda Romero, Maria Romero, David Roseberry, Corinne Sanders, Dolores Slosar, Joyce Smith, Sandy Smith, Marie and Emile de Tiege, Darcy Tom and Helen Zabawa.

Assisting Children to Live with Death

Adults must play a significant role in assisting children to live with death. The most important thing adults can do is to help children understand and accept their feelings throughout the entire death experience. The following information is intended to assist you in this effort.

1. Children need to learn how to mourn, that is, to go through the process of giving up some of the feelings they have invested in an animal or person and go on with other and new relationships. They need to remember, to be touched by the feelings generated by their memories. They need to struggle with real or imagined guilt over what they could have done. They need to deal with their anger over the loss.

2. Children need to mourn over the small losses, such as plants and animals, in order to deal better with larger, closer losses of people.

3. Children need to be informed about a death. If they aren't told but see that adults are upset, they may invent their own explanations and even blame themselves.

4. Children need to understand the finality of death. Because abstract thinking is difficult for them, they may misunderstand if adults say that a person or animal "went away" or "went to sleep." If you believe in an afterlife and want to tell your child about it, it is important to emphasize that he/she won't see the person or animal again on Earth.

5. Children need to say good-bye to the deceased by participating in viewings and/or funerals, if only for a few minutes. No child is too young to participate in these activities.

6. Children need opportunities to work out their feelings and deal with their perceptions of death by talking, dramatic playing, reading books or expressing themselves through the arts.

7. Children need reassurance that the adults in their lives will take care of themselves and probably won't die until after the children are grown. However, children need to know that everybody will die someday.

8. Children need to know that other children die, but only if they are very sick or if there is a bad accident. It is equally important that they understand that almost all children grow and live to be very old.

9. Children need to be allowed to show their feelings: to cry, become angry or even laugh. The best approach is to empathize with their feelings. For example, you might say, "You're sad. You miss Grandma. Tell me about it."

10. Children need to feel confident that their questions will be answered honestly and not avoided. They need to know that adults will give them answers they can understand. Adults should take their cues from the children and answer only what they ask.

GA1317

Developmental Stages

Children go through a series of stages in their understanding of death. Most children between the ages of 2 and 4 see death as reversible, temporary and impersonal. Watching television cartoon characters rise up miraculously after having been blown apart tends to reinforce this notion.

Between the ages of 5 and 9, most children begin to realize that death is final and that all living things die. They still do not see death as personal. They hold the notion that they can escape death through their own ingenuity and efforts.

From age 9 or 10 through adolescence, children begin to comprehend fully that death is irreversible, that all living things die, and that they too will die someday. Many teenagers become intrigued with seeking the meaning of life and developing philosophical views of life and death.

Time Intervals for Mourning

In helping older children deal with death, it may be important to be aware of critical time intervals related to mourning. Mourning is the process whereby children work through the death of a loved one, thus regaining a sense of balance in their lives. Mourning is a functional necessity, not a weakness. It is a form of healing. Adults need to create the opportunities for children to be able to share their needs with us so we can assist them in living with death.

During the first twenty-four to forty-eight hours, the impact of the reality of death occurs. For the next five to seven days, one may experience a mild depressive reaction to this reality. The next six to eight weeks is the most difficult adjustment period. The impact of the death of a loved one hits with acute symptoms of anxiety and depression such as loss of sleep, overeating or lack of appetite, weeping, fatigue, acute mood swings, and decreased ability to concentrate and remember.

At about three months, the mourning person may experience irritability and complaining, physical and verbal acting-out of anger and frustration, crying, and physical complaints such as headaches, backaches, diarrhea, etc. At about six months, depression is a common occurrence with repeated depression at about twelve months. From twelve to twenty-four months, the mourning person usually arrives at an acceptance of the death or a resolution of the grief. Mild recurrent depression is often associated with the anniversary of the death of a loved one. Years after the death of this person, mild depression often occurs on special dates such as birthdays and holidays. These feelings and critical time intervals related to the mourning process may vary considerably for different people.

GA1317

Pretest

Write about your knowledge of and feelings towards dying and death.

Note: Do not be concerned if your knowledge about death is limited and your feelings are unclear. It may be that you have given only limited thought and discussion to this topic. The activities in this book are intended to help you gain a clearer understanding of the meaning of death in your life.

1

GA1317

Looking Ahead

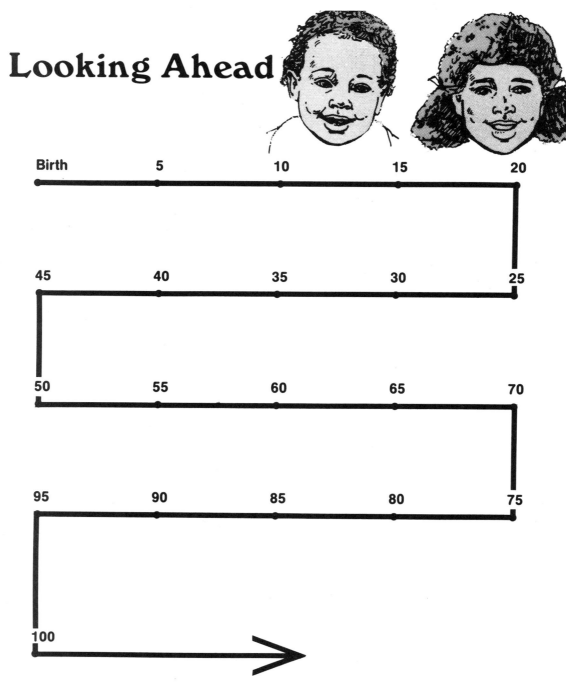

- Write your birth date above the word *birth*.

- Put a star (*) on the line at your present age.

- Put a question mark (?) at the age you expect to die.

- Write several things you have done in your lifetime and the age at which you accomplished each thing.

- Write several things you expect to do in your lifetime and the age at which you plan to accomplish each goal.

2

GA1317

Death History

1. The first death that I personally experienced was the death of

   _____

2. I was _____ years old.

3. At the time I felt _____

   _____

4. I was most curious about _____

   _____

5. The feelings that I have now when I think of this person's death are

   _____

   _____

   _____

   _____

6. My feelings when I think about my own death are _____

   _____

   _____

7. I believe I acquired these feelings about my death from _____

   _____

   _____

8. I think it is important to think about my death because (or, I do *not* think
   it is important to think about my death because)

   _____

   _____

GA1317

Reflecting on Life _____

1. To me, life is _____

_____

_____

2. I value life because _____

_____

_____

_____

3. The people and things I care most about in life are _____

_____

_____

_____

_____

_____

4. One change I would like to make in my life is _____

_____

_____

_____

5. One way I could live life more fully would be _____

_____

_____

_____

6. One thing I would like to have happen during my lifetime is _____

_____

_____

_____

GA1317

Reflecting on Death _____

Circle as many answers that accurately complete each statement for you.

1. I have personally experienced the death of
   a. a plant
   b. a pet
   c. a parent
   d. a grandparent or great-grandparent
   e. a brother or sister
   f. another family member
   g. a friend
   h. a stranger
   i. a public figure
   j. other: _____

2. The subject of dying is talked about in my family
   a. openly
   b. with some sense of discomfort
   c. only when necessary and then with an attempt to exclude me
   d. as very little as possible
   e. other: _____

3. If my doctor told my family that I had an illness and was going to die, I
   a. would want to be told
   b. would not want to be told

4. If someone close to me were dying and wanted to talk about it, I would feel
   a. uncomfortable and unwilling to talk
   b. uncomfortable but willing to talk
   c. at ease and willing to talk
   d. other: _____

5. When I think about my own death, I feel
   a. afraid
   b. discouraged or depressed
   c. at peace
   d. sort of excited about the prospect
   e. other: _____

6. When I am asked to attend the funeral of a person, I
   a. make excuses until I do not have to attend
   b. dislike it and wish I had never attended
   c. dislike it but later feel glad to have attended
   d. am grateful to be included and am happy to attend
   e. other: _____

GA1317

Depicting Life

Draw, photograph or find magazine words and pictures that depict *life*. Display your artwork in the space provided.

6

GA1317

Depicting
Death

Draw, photograph or find magazine words and pictures that depict *death*. Display your artwork in the space provided.

Purpose in Nature _____

Everything in life has a purpose. Choose two living things in nature. List reasons why these living things exist.

_____

_____

_____

_____

_____

_____

_____

_____

_____

_____

_____

_____

8

My Purpose in Life

Every person in life has a purpose. Paste a picture of yourself in the space. List your purposes for living. Put a star (★) next to your most important purpose in life.

GA1317

Cycles of Life

Nature teaches about the cycles of life. Every living thing has a birth, growth and death cycle. For example, a seed sprouts and grows into a flower that produces more seeds for new life. Then the flower dies and decomposes into the earth to offer nourishment for other seeds to grow.

Find signs of birth, growth and death in nature. Write your observations below.

Signs of Birth	Signs of Growth	Signs of Death

10

GA1317

Life After Death

When a person dies, his/her body becomes a part of nature's cyclical process. The body decomposes and returns to the earth.

Many people believe in a life after death. They believe that the soul, or spirit, or thoughts, or love of the dead person lives on in some way.

Discuss the possibility of life after death with your family and friends. Tell why you believe or do not believe in a life after death or why you have no clear opinion on this subject at this time.

_____

_____

_____

_____

_____

_____

_____

_____

_____

_____

_____

_____

_____

_____

_____

_____

_____

GA1317

Death of a Pet

The death of a pet is often a difficult loss to experience.

Tell about the life of your pet.

_____

_____

_____

_____

Tell about the death of your pet.

_____

_____

_____

_____

Tell how you felt at the death of your pet.

_____

_____

_____

_____

_____

_____

_____

_____

_____

GA1317

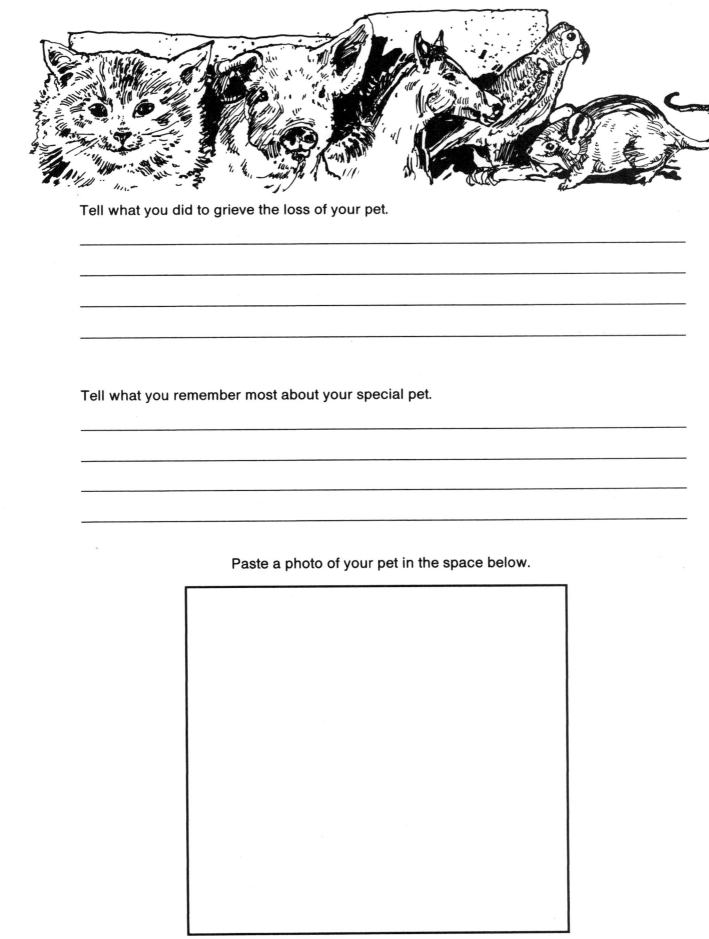

Tell what you did to grieve the loss of your pet.

_____

_____

_____

_____

Tell what you remember most about your special pet.

_____

_____

_____

_____

Paste a photo of your pet in the space below.

Share with a friend the life and death of your pet.

13

GA1317

In Loving Memory

Ask your Mom and/or Dad to tell you about the life and death of a relative you never knew. Paste a picture of this person in the space below. Tell about this person in the space below.

14

Remembering the Dead

Has someone in your family or very close to you died? If so, tell about this person.

_____

_____

_____

_____

What is the best memory you have of this person?

_____

_____

_____

_____

_____

How did you deal with the loss of the physical presence of this person in your life?

_____

_____

_____

_____

_____

15

GA1317

Beliefs About Death

Circle *YES* if you *agree* with the statement. Circle *NO* if you *disagree* with the statement. Circle *UNCERTAIN* if you have no *clear opinion* about the statement.

a. Death is only for old people and sick people to think about.   YES   NO   UNCERTAIN

b. Death is a result of evil in the world.   YES   NO   UNCERTAIN

c. It is possible to fear life more than death.   YES   NO   UNCERTAIN

d. There is a life after death.   YES   NO   UNCERTAIN

e. Death is a new beginning rather than a final ending.   YES   NO   UNCERTAIN

f. When a relative or friend dies, I must somehow accept the loss of the physical presence of this person in my life.   YES   NO   UNCERTAIN

g. I can have many feelings about the death of a person I love (anger, discouragement, relief, sadness, peace).   YES   NO   UNCERTAIN

h. Living with death is a normal part of life.   YES   NO   UNCERTAIN

i. Adults should protect children from dealing with death experiences.   YES   NO   UNCERTAIN

j. The best way to prepare for death is to live a life of love.   YES   NO   UNCERTAIN

GA1317

Taking a Survey

Ask five friends to define *death*. Write their definitions below.

Death is _____
_____
_____
_____

Death is _____
_____
_____
_____

Death is _____
_____
_____

Death is _____
_____
_____
_____

Death is _____
_____
_____
_____

Write your own definition of *death* below.

Death is _____
_____
_____
_____

GA1317

Stages of Dying

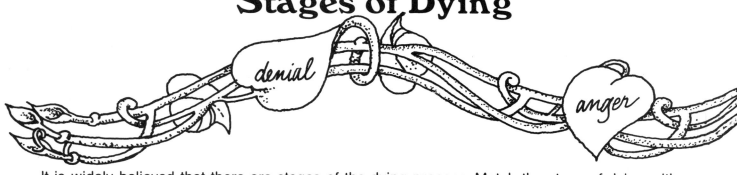

It is widely believed that there are stages of the dying process. Match the stage of dying with the feeling a dying person might have at that particular time in the death process.

1. denial

a. "If I get cured, I'm going to spend the rest of my life doing good things for other people."

2. anger

b. "I can't be sick. The doctor's test must be wrong."

3. bargaining

c. "I can't die. I'm too young and I have too much work to do. It just isn't fair."

4. depression

d. "I don't know how long I will live, but I have today, and I'm going to live it to the fullest."

5. acceptance

e. "Why should I bother to take better care of myself? Nothing I do will make me well."

People who suffer the loss and death of a person they love also go through the five stages of the dying process. Match the stage of dying with the feeling a relative of the dying person might have.

1. denial	a. "If she dies, I have nothing to live for. I might as well die, too."
2. anger	b. "It just can't be! She's never been sick a day in her life."
3. bargaining	c. "I'll try to make every remaining moment count. After she dies I'll pick up the pieces of my life and put them back together somehow."
4. depression	d. "Life is so unfair. Why does this have to happen to our family?"
5. acceptance	e. "I wish we could change places. Let her get well and let me be sick."

Note: Reprinted with permission from Elisabeth Kubler-Ross, *On Death and Dying.* Copyright © 1969, Macmillan Publishing Company.

Knowing My Feelings

Below are feelings that might be expressed by a child whose parent is dying of a serious disease. Indicate the stage of death (denial, anger, bargaining, depression, acceptance) that the child may be experiencing.

1. _____ "If my mom gets better, I will never fight with my little brother again."

2. _____ "The doctors are wrong. I am sure my mom will get better."

3. _____ "My mom has been suffering for a long time. When she dies she will be out of pain."

4. _____ "I will never love again so I can never be hurt again."

5. _____ "My mom is too sick to play with me and drive me places. I wish I had a different mom."

6. _____ "If Dad marries after Mom dies, I will never love my new mom. I wish I could die, too."

7. _____ "This can't be true. I know a cure will be found soon."

8. _____ "We will miss Mom a lot, but we will get along somehow."

9. _____ "I am very upset that Mom doesn't spend time with me like she used to. It just isn't fair."

10. _____ "I will pray for a miracle, and Mom will be cured."

GA1317

A Death Experience _____

Life has many death experiences where one feels disbelief, anger, guilt and acceptance, etc. Going through a divorce may be a death experience. Moving from an old neighborhood to a new neighborhood may be a death experience. Breaking an arm may be a death experience.

Think about a "death experience" you may have had. Write about your experience below.

_____

_____

_____

_____

_____

_____

_____

_____

_____

_____

_____

_____

_____

_____

_____

_____

_____

You may want to talk about this death experience with a person whom you love and trust.

Recognizing Feelings_____

Below are initial feelings that a child might have upon the death of a parent. Write *yes* in front of the feelings that you might have and *no* in front of the feelings you probably would not have. Remember, there are no wrong or right feelings.

_____   "I don't feel anything. I don't even feel like crying."

_____   "I feel relieved because things will be better now."

_____   "I feel scared because something might happen to my other parent."

_____   "I feel angry because this shouldn't have happened to me."

_____   "I feel peaceful because my mom (or dad) is at peace."

_____   "I feel angry because everyone is making decisions for me."

Make up your own feelings below.

I feel _____ because _____

_____

_____

I feel_____ because_____

_____

_____

22

Saying What You Want to Hear _____

When someone dies, adults usually behave in ways that they were taught. Listed below are some things that adults might say at the death of a relative or friend. Write *yes* in the box if you would like the sentence said to you and *no* in the box if you would not like the sentence said to you.

☐ "Don't cry. I know you will help by being very strong and brave."

☐ "This is a very sad thing that has happened to us. We need to cry together."

☐ "There are many people in the house. Maybe you should go and play in your bedroom."

☐ "You might want to stay and hear all the good things people say about the person we love very much."

☐ "We are going to the funeral home. Do you want to come along?"

☐ "We are going to the funeral home. You stay home so you will remember him/her alive, not dead."

What would you like adults to say to you at the death of a relative or friend?

_____

_____

_____

_____

_____

_____

_____

_____

23

Living Better—Not Longer_____

Imagine being told that you have six months to a year to live. How would you feel? Shocked? Angry? Sad? Depressed? Envious of those who will live on after you? Would you lose interest in life? Would you become more aware of life?

Tell how you would feel and what you would do if you had six months or a year to live.

_____

_____

_____

_____

_____

_____

_____

_____

_____

_____

_____

_____

_____

_____

_____

_____

_____

_____

_____

_____

GA1317

Living Today _____

If you had only five days to live, how would you spend these days? With whom would you spend these days?

_____

_____

_____

_____

_____

_____

_____

_____

_____

_____

_____

_____

_____

_____

_____

_____

_____

_____

_____

_____

Why wait? You may want to make your five dream days a reality now.

GA1317

Death: A Natural Part of Life _____

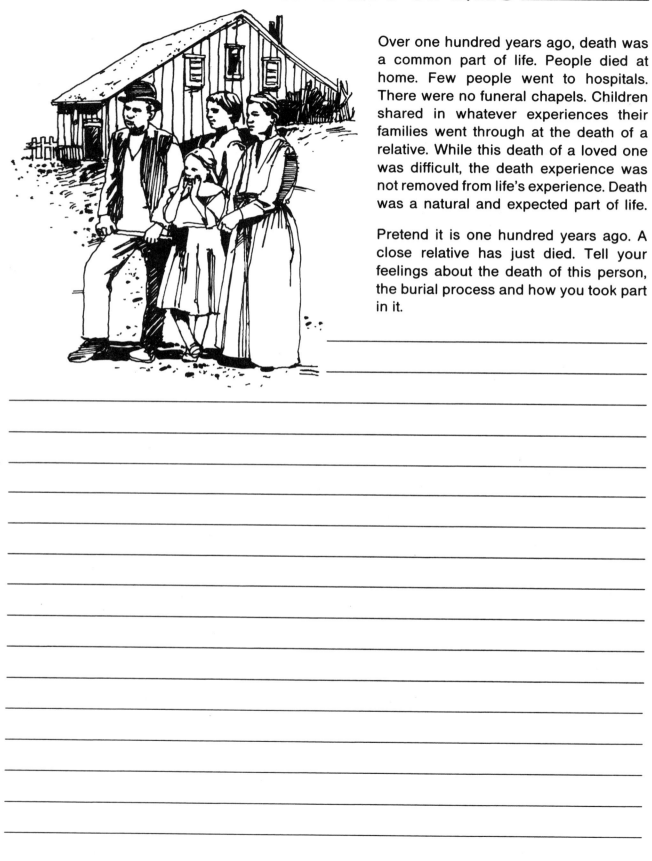

Over one hundred years ago, death was a common part of life. People died at home. Few people went to hospitals. There were no funeral chapels. Children shared in whatever experiences their families went through at the death of a relative. While this death of a loved one was difficult, the death experience was not removed from life's experience. Death was a natural and expected part of life.

Pretend it is one hundred years ago. A close relative has just died. Tell your feelings about the death of this person, the burial process and how you took part in it.

26

Death: An Unnatural Part of Life

Science has changed things in the past one hundred years. Operations and childbirth are safer. We have better nutrition. Immunizations have eliminated many contagious diseases. Our lives are longer and healthier.

Gradually, death has become more removed from daily life. Deaths are seen and talked about less and less. People have become less comfortable with death as it has become less a part of our daily living.

Pretend that a close friend has just died. Tell what your feelings might be and how you might take part in the burial process.

_____

_____

_____

_____

_____

_____

_____

_____

_____

_____

_____

_____

_____

_____

_____

_____

GA1317

Cultural Burial Customs

Though customs differ, people the world over show sorrow and grief when a loved one dies. Match the group of people with their burial customs. You may need to research the burial customs of the people listed below.

1. Navajo Indians

a. The family helps the dying person depart by laying the person on a bed of straw on the ground so that he/she may be free from knots that entangle the soul and body. When death occurs, the family liberates the soul by opening all the doors and windows, and sometimes removing the roof.

2. Australians

b. These people are afraid of the spirits of the dead. Relatives prepare the body and bury it in an out-of-the-way place. Each person returns home in a roundabout way so the spirit of the dead person will not follow. Then the mourners stand in the smoke of an open fire to purify themselves.

3. Polish Peasants

c. Cremation is practiced. The body is carried to a burning ghat—a level area on a riverbank close to a temple. There the body is burned on a pile of logs, and the ashes are scattered onto the river.

4. Indians and South Asians

d. The body is often dressed in silk gowns or night attire. With few exceptions, the deceased is buried in an eight foot by four-foot grave that holds two or three coffins.

28

GA1317

Picturing Life After Death _____

Many people believe that within each person (and perhaps in animals, plants, rocks and rivers) there is a *spirit*. This spirit or *soul* can exist separately from the body. Some people believe the soul goes to a spirit land, sometimes called Paradise or Heaven, where perfect happiness exists. Some people believe that a spirit leaves a dying person and enters the body of a baby that is being born. Other people believe that a human spirit finds a home in some animal— a bird, a cow or a dog. These beliefs of a spirit living again in another person or animal are called *reincarnation*.

If you believe in a life after death, use words and pictures to describe what you think this might be like.

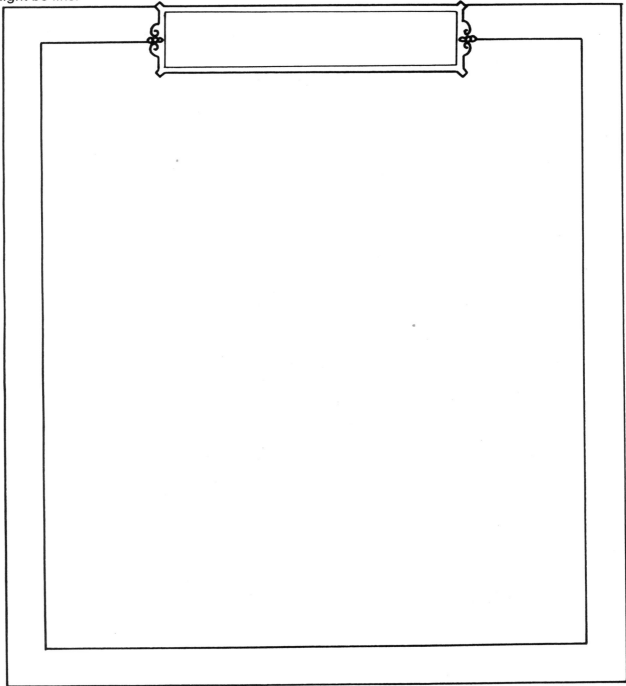

GA1317

Expected Presence _____

When a person is living, you can expect his/her presence in your life. You can expect to relate to this person in a specific way. Tell how you relate to a living person who is special to you. Describe the *physical presence* of this person: how the person looks, sounds, feels, smells, moves, etc.

_____

_____

_____

_____

_____

_____

_____

_____

_____

                              _____

                              _____

                              _____

                              _____

                              _____

                              _____

                              _____

                              _____

                              _____

GA1317

Unlearning Expected Presence _____

When a person you love dies, there is sorrow because you can no longer relate to this person the way you did when he/she was living. You have to unlearn this person's expected physical presence in your life.

a. Tell about a time when you had to unlearn the expected presence of someone you loved very much. Tell how you learned to relate to this person in a new, nonphysical way.

b. Write what you remember about a person you loved very much who has died. Tell about the physical qualities of this person, but also tell about the nonphysical qualities of this person, such as gentleness, honesty, etc.

GA1317

Visiting a Mortuary

Visit a mortuary. A mortuary is also called a funeral home.

- Ask the mortician to explain the purpose of his/her job.

- Visit the various rooms of the mortuary. Listen to the explanation of the purpose of each room.

- Ask the mortician to explain the purpose and process of cremation, in which the body is burned and the ashes are usually buried.

- Ask the mortician to tell you about funeral preparations and expenses.

- Tell about your trip to the mortuary below.

_____

_____

_____

_____

_____

_____

_____

_____

_____

_____

_____

_____

_____

_____

_____

_____

GA1317

Paying for a Funeral

Below are the expense items for a funeral. Each item has an actual or varied cost. Determine the total cost of your own funeral and burial in the space provided.

Earth Burial Costs

Cemetery lot	$525-2250
Caskets	$285-6000
Mortician fee	$473-1227
Concrete casket liner	$368
Vault	$8600
Gravesite costs	$385
Tombstone	$405-2000

Cremation Costs

Preparation of the body	$473
Cremation fees	$125
Cremation box	$80
Urn	$10-500

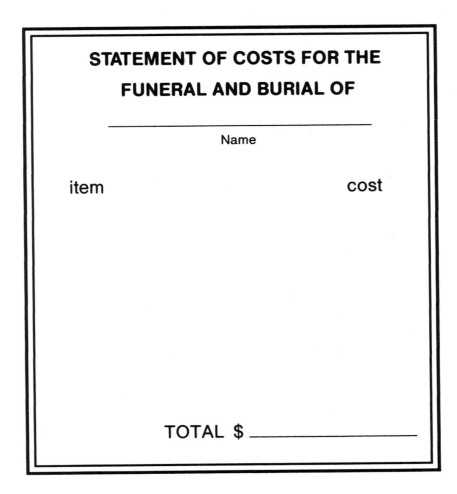

STATEMENT OF COSTS FOR THE

FUNERAL AND BURIAL OF

_____

Name

item   cost

TOTAL $ _____

Note: People who die without money and without friends or relatives are buried by the community welfare agency. The burial ground for these people is called Potter's Field, the name of the burial place provided long ago for strangers at the city of Jerusalem.

Visiting a Cemetery

a. Go to a cemetery. Ask the proprietor of the cemetery to explain the purpose of his/her job. What are the jobs of other people who work at the cemetery?

b. Improve the appearance of the cemetery or a particular gravesite in some way.

c. While visiting the cemetery, observe the types of tombstones and read the various epitaphs. An epitaph is an inscription on a tombstone in memory of the person buried there. Write, in the space below, an epitaph you observed.

_____

_____

_____

_____

_____

_____

d. Write an imaginary story about the life of this person.

_____

_____

_____

_____

_____

_____

_____

_____

_____

_____

_____

GA1317

Designing Your Tombstone

Design your own tombstone. Write your epitaph on your tombstone.

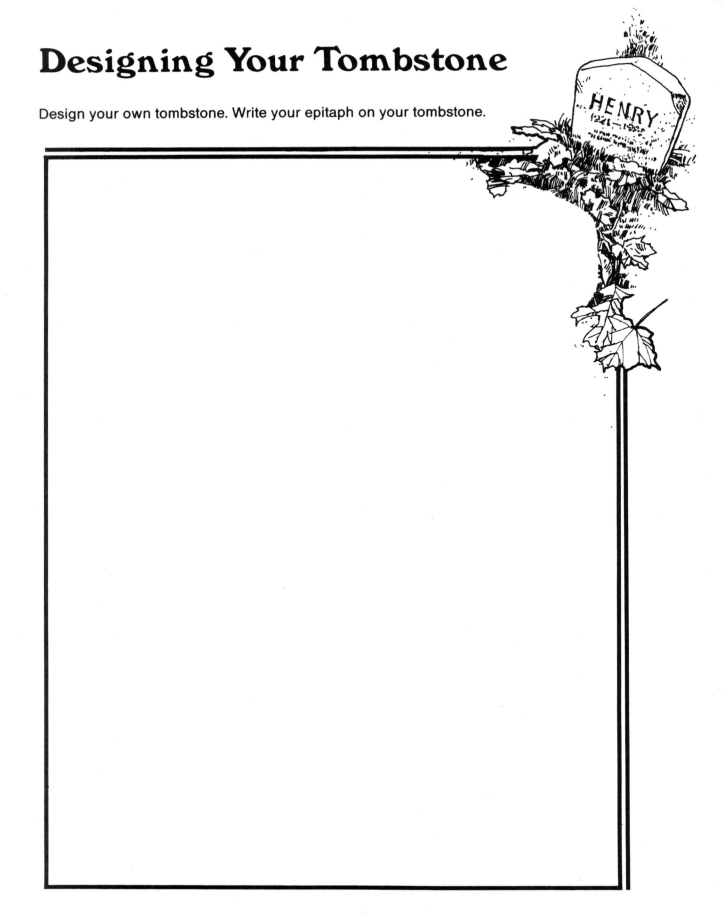

GA1317

Obituaries

An obituary is a notice of a person's death, usually with a short account of the life of the person.

Read the obituary column in the newspaper. Cut out some obituaries of interest to you and paste them below.

GA1317

Write your own obituary in the space below.

_____

_____

_____

_____

_____

_____

_____

_____

_____

_____

_____

_____

_____

_____

_____

_____

_____

_____

_____

In Memory of

It is sometimes customary in this country for the family of the deceased person to request that donations be made to a specific organization or place of interest to them rather than have their friends spend money on flowers to be sent to the mortuary as a sign of their love and support.

For what would you like your friends to spend money in your memory?

_____

_____

_____

_____

_____

Why would you like your friends to give money in your memory in this way?

_____

_____

_____

_____

_____

_____

_____

_____

You might want to tell a parent, relative, or friend that you have this desire. Have you included information in your obituary on the previous page?

Wills

A will is a written document whereby a person bequeaths or gives away his/her worldly possessions as he/she chooses. Children are often the beneficiaries of their parents' wills. This means, at the death of both parents, the child or children would have ownership of the material possessions of their parents. Wills are usually complicated legal documents that need the assistance of a lawyer to be written properly. Some people make unofficial verbal or written wills. This can be done by telling a friend informally or by writing how you want your possessions to be used after your death. In such cases your wishes will probably be respected if your possessions are not of great monetary value.

Make an informal will below. List those possessions of value to you. List items that are important to you even though they may not be worth a lot of money. Name who should receive these items at the time of your death.

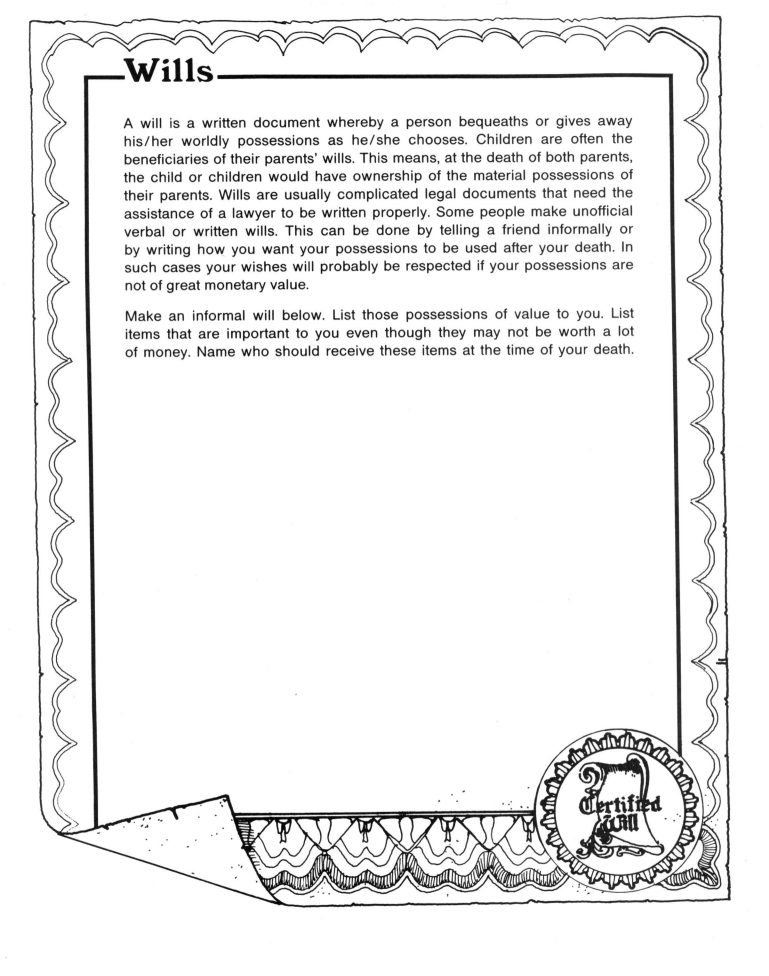

GA1317

Rights of a Dying Person

A dying person has the right:

- to be treated as a living person

- to be cared for by kind, sensitive people

- to be hopeful and to be cared for by hopeful people

- to participate in decisions about his/her care

- to have his/her questions answered honestly

- to the truth, even without asking questions

- to be free from pain

- to seek comfort rather than a cure

- to express feelings and emotions about his/her death

- to have help in accepting his/her death

- to die with family and friends present

- to maintain his/her own spiritual beliefs regarding death and dying

- to die in dignity and peace

- to have his/her body respected after death

- Discuss the rights of a dying person with an adult whom you respect.

- Add more rights that you believe belong to a dying person.

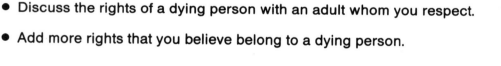

_____

_____

_____

_____

_____

_____

_____

_____

_____

Unfinished Business

"Unfinished business" are those things that you still have to think, say, feel or do to replace the negative aspects of your life with positive love. If you have negative feelings about a person, you have unfinished business. If you have unfinished business with a person, you often feel guilty when this person dies. You regret that you did not resolve your differences with this person by replacing the negative aspects of your relationship with positive love.

- Identify the unfinished business in your life. Identify those things that keep you from thinking and acting in a positive, loving way.

- Share your plan to resolve your unfinished business with an adult who really cares about you.

- Make peace with yourself and others by completing your unfinished business.

- If appropriate, tell about your unfinished business and plan for improvement in the space below.

_____

_____

_____

_____

_____

_____

A person may deeply regret not completing unfinished business before the death of a loved one. If this is true for you, it is not too late to improve your relationship with the person who has died. One way this can be done is by writing all the things that you wish you had told this special person in your life. When you are certain that your message is clear and complete, burn the letter with the intention of uniting your thoughts with the spirit of the person you love. Continue to let go of any further regrets you may have concerning your past relationship with this person. (If you do not believe in a spirit in life and/or in death, you can unite your past love for this person in life with your present love for this person in death.)

Note: You may want to mix the ashes of your letter with soil. This will provide a rich soil for the growth of plants.

Euthanasia

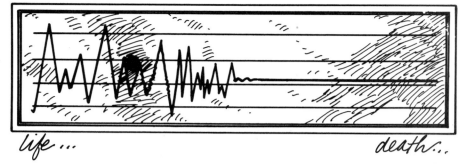

life ...   *death ...*

Euthanasia is the act of ending the life of a person thought to be incurably ill or injured in order to spare the person further suffering. Below are statements that agree and disagree with the practice of euthanasia. Determine whether each statement is *for* or *against* the practice of euthanasia. Circle your answers below.

"For a terminally ill person, a doctor has the duty to relieve suffering more than maintain life."   FOR   AGAINST

"It is a doctor's duty to save life, not destroy it."   FOR   AGAINST

"A disease or condition considered incurable today may be curable tomorrow. Wait for the cure."   FOR   AGAINST

"It is highly unlikely that there will be a medical discovery capable of undoing the irreversible damage for a person who already has a terminal illness."   FOR   AGAINST

"Only God has the right to determine when life should end. People must not play God."   FOR   AGAINST

"The Bible says, 'Blessed are the merciful.' To end the hopeless suffering of a dying person would be a merciful act."   FOR   AGAINST

"Powerful, pain-killing drugs allow people to die in peace and comfort."   FOR   AGAINST

"Pain-killing drugs do not always keep a dying person comfortable. And besides, there are other factors, such as difficult breathing, weakness, paralysis, loss of memory, etc., with which a dying person might have to deal."   FOR   AGAINST

Do you generally agree or disagree with the practice of euthanasia?

Give reasons to support your personal viewpoints regarding this complex issue in the space below.

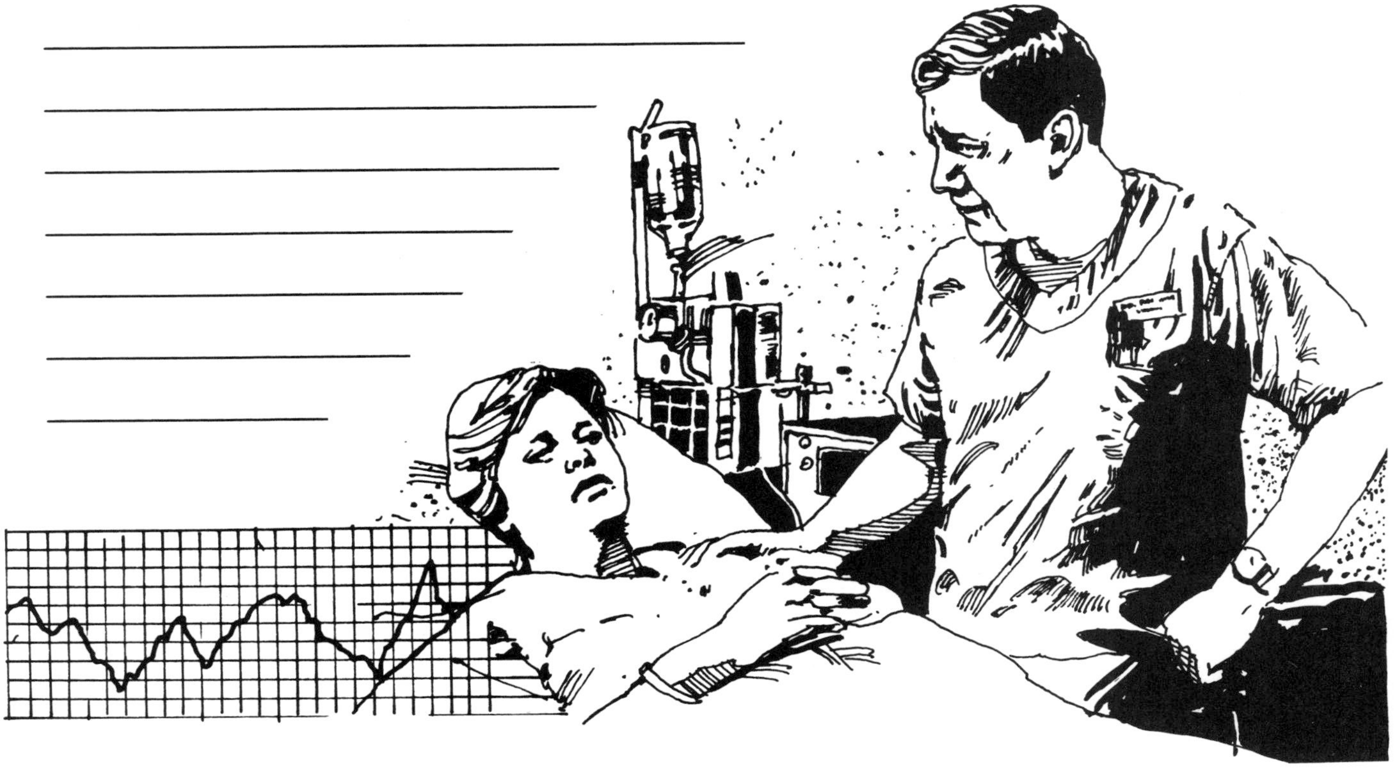

_____

_____

_____

_____

_____

_____

_____

_____

_____

_____

_____

_____

_____

_____

_____

_____

_____

_____

_____

_____

_____

GA1317

Suicide

When a person ends his or her own life, it is called suicide. When a person commits suicide it is very hard to believe that this death is caused by an illness. Some people get physically sick and their lives end. Other people get mentally sick and end their lives. When a person commits suicide, it means he/she is too mentally ill to go on living.

For a suicidal person, life is no longer worth living. What is most important in life is missing, destroyed and unattainable. There is more pain than pleasure. There are feelings of helplessness and powerlessness. The inability to sort out positive solutions and choices for the future leads to feelings of frustration, confusion and depression. The person sees death as the only way out of the dilemma.

Ask people from a local suicide prevention center to talk with you about their work. Ask them to tell how some suicides can be prevented. Write what you learned from the conversation in the space below.

_____

_____

_____

_____

_____

_____

_____

_____

_____

_____

_____

_____

_____

_____

_____

_____

_____

_____

GA1317

Getting Help

It is natural to feel sad and unhappy for a long time when someone you love very much dies. But sometimes you think about dying so much that you cannot seem to get on with living. Sometimes you need help to sort out your feelings about life and death.

a. Listed below are people who might be able to help you sort out these feelings. Put a check (✓) before the people you feel could help you clarify your feelings about life, dying and death.

_____	a good friend	_____	a nurse
_____	a parent	_____	a teacher
_____	a relative	_____	a counselor
_____	a neighbor	_____	a doctor
_____	a minister, priest or rabbi		
_____	other: _____		

b. Look in the phone book to see if there are any groups to help people deal with dying and death. Write the names, addresses and phone numbers of some of these organizations below.

_____   _____

_____   _____

_____   _____

Ask one or more of these people to explain how they help other people to live with death.

GA1317

Donating Organs _____

Some people believe that they can improve the quality of life for others by donating their body parts at the time of their death. Some people donate their eyes, kidneys, liver, heart, etc., that others might live healthier, happier lives. If you would like to donate your body organs at the time of your death, fill out the information below. Give a copy of this document to a member of your immediate family so this person will be aware of your desire and request.

UNIFORM DONOR CERTIFICATE

. of _____
                    Name of Donor

In the hope that I may help others, I hereby make this gift of my body, if medically acceptable, to take effect upon my death. The words and marks below indicate my desires.

For the purposes of transplantation and therapy:

☐ I give any needed organs or parts.

☐ I give only the following specified organs or parts:

_____

For the purposes of medical research and education:

☐ I give my body, if needed.

Limitations or special wishes, if any: _____

Signed by the donor and the following two witnesses in the presence of each other:

_____	_____
Signature of Donor	Signature of Witness
_____	_____
Date of Birth of Donor	Signature of Witness
_____	_____
City, State, Zip	Date

This is a legal document under the Uniform Anatomical Gift Act or similar laws.

You may want to have this document witnessed by a notary public.

Making a Living Will ───────────

Dying people have the right to participate in all decisions concerning their care. Many people express these rights through living wills that others must enforce even if the dying person is too sick or unable to speak on his/her own behalf. Below is a standard sample of a living will. It may be appropriate to have your living will reviewed and approved by a lawyer to assure that it meets all legal requirements.

A LIVING WILL

To my family
To any medical facility in whose care I happen to be
To any individual who may become responsible for my health, welfare or affairs,

Death is as much a reality as birth, growth, maturity and old age—it is the one certainty of life. If the time comes when I, _____ can no longer take part in any decisions for my own future, let this statement stand as an expression of my wishes, while I am still of sound mind.

If the situation should arise in which there is no reasonable expectation of my recovery from physical or mental disability, I request that I be allowed to die and not be kept alive by artificial means or heroic measures. I do not fear death itself as much as the indignities of deterioration, dependence and hopeless pain. I, therefore, ask that medication be mercifully administered to me to alleviate suffering even though this may hasten the moment of death.

This request is made after careful consideration. I hope you who care for me will feel morally bound to follow this mandate. I recognize that this appears to place a heavy responsibility upon you, but it is with the intention of relieving you of such responsibility and of placing it upon myself in accordance with my strong convictions that this statement is made.

Signed _____

Date _____

Witnessed by: _____

Date _____

Witnessed by: _____

Date _____

 GA1317

Summary

48

Across

4. The act of intentionally killing oneself

6. The act of making a trade with a higher power (God) in order to save the life of the dying person

8. A feeling of deep sadness over the death of a person

9. The ceremony held in connection with the burial or cremation of the dead

10. The period of time between birth and death

11. A feeling of being mad about the death of a person you love

13. A printed notice of a person's death

15. Casket; the case that holds the body of a dead person

16. Graveyard; a place for burying the dead

17. The writing on a tombstone in memory of the person buried there

18. A place where dead bodies are prepared or kept before burial or cremation

19. The burning of the dead body to ashes

20. A legal document of how a person wishes his/her possessions to be given away after his/her death

Down

1. Those things that you still have to say or do to improve the quality of your life

2. A person who could help you sort out your feelings related to a death experience

3. Mercy killing; the act of killing a person thought to be incurably ill or injured in order to spare this person from suffering

5. Believing that death will not or did not happen

7. The final stage of mourning whereby one understands and agrees with the fact that a loved one has died

8. The end of physical life

12. The belief that the spirit or soul of a dead person lives on in another person or animal

14. Spirit; the spiritual nature of a person; the force that gives life to a body

GA1317

Ten Guidelines for Living with Death

1. **ACCEPT YOUR SORROW.** Do not try to be brave. Take time to cry. Crying is not a sign of lack of strength. It is a natural expression of sorrow.

2. **TALK ABOUT IT.** Find a family member or friend to talk to. Your friends may act embarrassed at first. You can help them and you by talking about the death of your loved one. Find someone who has experienced a similar sorrow. Talk often.

3. **KEEP BUSY.** Do purposeful work that occupies your mind. Avoid frantic activity.

4. **EAT WELL.** Your body needs good nourishment during this time of emotional and physical loss. A vitamin supplement might be helpful.

5. **EXERCISE REGULARLY.** Depression can be lessened by body changes brought on by exercise. Exercise will also help you sleep better. Return to your old exercise program or start a new program as soon as possible.

6. **ACCEPT YOUR UNDERSTANDING OF THE DEATH.** You have probably asked "why" over and over and have gotten no satisfying answer to your question. You probably have some small degree of understanding. Accept this viewpoint until you are able to have a deeper understanding of this experience. Some questions have no satisfying answers.

7. **GIVE OF YOURSELF.** Find a way to help others. Helping to ease someone else's pain will probably lessen your own.

8. **KEEP A JOURNAL.** Recording your thoughts in a journal may help you get your feelings out. Your journal may also serve as a vehicle to record your progress.

9. **SEEK INNER STRENGTH.** Get in touch with the source of your inner strength. Set aside time to find peace of mind. If you value religion, stay active in your church. Scripture has much to say about sorrow. As time passes, you will feel less abandoned. You will find peace through God or that source of strength and power bigger than yourself.

10. **GET HELP.** Don't let your sorrow cripple you. There comes a time to stop crying and get on with your life. Sometimes a trained counselor may help you get over your anger, guilt and sorrow that keep you from becoming a happier person.

GA1317

Posttest

Write about your knowledge and feelings toward dying and death.

Compare these thoughts and feelings with those described in the pretest before you began the activities in this book.

After completing the activities in this book,

my knowledge of death is

☐ greater

☐ less

☐ about the same

my feelings about death are

☐ clearer

☐ less clear

☐ about the same

Vocabulary

ACCEPTANCE—The final stage of mourning whereby one understands and agrees with the fact that a loved one has died

ANGER—A feeling of hostility (being mad) about the death of a person you love

BARGAINING—A stage in accepting death whereby a person tries to make a trade with a higher power (God) in order to save the life of the dying person

CASKET—Coffin; the case that holds the body of a dead person

CEMETERY—Graveyard; a place for burying the dead

CREMATION—The burning of the corpse (dead body) to ashes

CYCLE—A regularly repeated series of events (such as the changing of the seasons)

DEATH—The end of physical life

DENIAL—The first stage in accepting death whereby the person tries to believe that death will not or did not happen

DEPRESSION—A feeling of deep sadness over the death of a person

EPITAPH—The writing on a tombstone in memory of the person buried there

EUTHANASIA—Mercy killing; the act of killing a person thought to be incurably ill or injured in order to spare this person from suffering

FUNERAL—The ceremony held in connection with the burial or cremation of the dead

LIFE—The period of time between birth and death

LIVING WILL—A document written by a well person instructing others how this person wishes to be treated when he/she is dying

MORTICIAN—A funeral director; an undertaker

MORTUARY—A place where dead bodies are prepared or kept before burial or cremation

OBITUARY—A printed notice of a person's death

REINCARNATION—The belief that the spirit or soul of a dead person lives on in another person or animal

SOUL—Spirit; the spiritual nature of a person; the force that gives life to a body

SUICIDE—The act of intentionally killing oneself

WILL—A legal document of how a person wishes his/her possessions to be given away after his/her death

GA1317

Final Note to Students

Death teaches you about love. The death of a person hurts so much because of your love for that special person. It hurts a lot because you love a lot. The heartbreak of having this person die teaches you how valuable and unique this person was. You can, of course, find other people to love, but each new love is special and different.

Death teaches you about life. Nobody ever dies completely. Every person who has ever lived has added to the world in a small or large way. Every person leaves the kindnesses and love offered to his/her immediate family and his/her world family, for we are all one planet and one people. Each person leaves the good deeds of his/her talents and works. He/She lives on in the hearts and memories of the people who knew and loved him/her. The person who has died will be a part of you all of your life, for he/she will forever live in your mind and heart.

And you, too, are daily offering love and good deeds to your immediate and world families. When you die, your love will continue to live on in the lives of those you have loved. That is why it is important that you concern yourself with living and loving rather than dying. You prepare to die by living life to its fullest. You prepare to die by filling your life with love. When you die, LOVE is all you leave behind in this life you are presently living. LOVE is all you take into your next state of being.

It is my sincerest hope that the activities in this book have given you a better understanding of death and a greater commitment to a life of love.

Peace always—

Judy Bisegnano

GA1317

Answer Key

STAGES OF DYING
Page 18: 1. b, 2. c, 3. a, 4. e, 5. d
Page 19: 1. b, 2. d, 3. e, 4. a, 5. c

Note: Since depression is a form of anger, it may be difficult for some students to distinguish between these two feelings.

KNOWING MY FEELINGS Page 20
1. bargaining
2. denial
3. acceptance
4. depression
5. anger
6. depression
7. denial
8. acceptance
9. anger
10. bargaining

CULTURAL BURIAL CUSTOMS Page 28
1. b, 2. a, 3. d, 4. c

SUMMARY CROSSWORD Page 48
Across
4. suicide
6. bargaining
8. depression
9. funeral
10. life
11. anger
13. obituary
15. coffin
16. cemetery
17. epitaph
18. mortuary
19. cremation
20. will

Down
1. unfinished business
2. counselor
3. euthanasia
5. denial
7. acceptance
8. death
12. reincarnation
14. soul

GA1317

Bibliography

It is often easier for younger children to read stories about the death of a plant or animal and then progress to books about the death of a person. The following annotated bibliography is divided into three parts: books written for children between the ages of 3 and 7, books written for children between the ages of 8 and 14, and books written for teenagers and adults. A complete bibliography is presented in an effort to assist varying aged members of a family—not just the person using this activity book as a personal journey for growth.

Books on death and dying can provide children with answers to questions that they may not know how to ask. Books can also provide the impetus for children to reveal their own thoughts and feelings as well as provide the framework for adult-child discussions about dying and death.

Before introducing a book about death to a child, it is very important that the teacher or parent first read the book. Familiarity with the book will assist the adult in answering questions a child may have. It will also allow the adult to determine if a book's content is consistent with one's own belief and approach to death—if such consistency is a necessary adult value.

Books for Children Ages 3 to 7

Aliki. The Two of Them. New York: Greenwillow Books, 1979.
> Called "A Poem of a Picture Book." The author captures true, lasting love of a grandparent and child in the markings of time—of life and death. A poem of meaning for adults and children to share together.

Buscaglia, Leo. *Freddie the Leaf.* Holt, Rinehart and Winston, 1982.
> A delightful book whereby Freddie compares the seasons of the year with the life-death cycle. Not until Freddie falls from the tree does he realize the fullness of the life he has had.

Carrick, Carol. *The Accident.* New York: Clarion Books, 1976.
> The accident wasn't anyone's fault, but at first Christopher blamed the driver who hit Bodger. Later he blamed himself. But no matter whom he blamed, nothing would bring Bodger back.

Cohn, Janice. *I Had a Friend Named Peter.* Wm. Morris & Co., Inc., 1987.
> A sensitive story about the accidental death of a little girl's best friend, and the parents and teacher who help her to understand what has happened. Includes a parent/teacher guide to answering children's questions about dying, funerals and the burial process.

Coutant, Helen. *First Snow.* New York: Alfred A. Knopf Publishers, 1974.
> A six-year-old Vietnamese girl, Lein, learns the meaning of death during her first snow. With the help of her grandmother, Lein begins to understand death as a natural part of life.

DePaola, Tomie. *Nana Upstairs, and Nana Downstairs.* New York: G. P. Putnam's Sons, 1973.
> Told in simple language and very readable to young preschoolers, this is a pictured example of caring for and looking after the very old. When death comes, a little boy learns its meaning.

GA1317

Graeber, Charlotte. *Mustard.* New York: Macmillan Publishing Company, 1982.
> When the vet diagnoses a heart ailment in Mustard the cat, eight-year-old Alex, with the help of his family, must come to terms with Mustard's increasing infirmities and eventual death.

Kubler-Ross, Elisabeth. *A Letter to a Child with Cancer.* Escondido, California: Shanti Nilaya, 1979.
> The author writes to a nine-year-old boy with cancer and answers his three questions: What is life? What is death? Why do young children have to die?

_____. *Remember the Secret.* Millbrae, California: Celestial Arts, 1982.
> Suzy and Peter are best friends with each other and their two unseen companions. Suzy is faced with the reality of Peter's death. When he joins their supposedly imaginary companions, there is sadness, but also wisdom and victory.

Miles, Misaka. *Annie and the Old One.* Little, Brown and Company, 1971.
> A beautiful story of a little Navajo Indian girl, Annie, who is given a weaving stick by her grandmother. Annie's grandmother is old and predicts that she will die and "return to mother earth" when the rug has been woven. To postpone her grandmother's death, Annie undoes the weaving already done. Her grandmother explains that one cannot change the order of nature and Annie begins to weave again.

Nobisson, Josephine. *Grandpa Loved.* San Diego: The Green Tiger Press, Inc., 1989.
> The boy tells how Grandpa loved the beach and showed the boy how to love it, too. The same with the wind, the woods, the animals, the city, the people and especially the family. When death comes, the boy concludes that Grandpa can go anywhere and see anything—the wind, the animals, the people and the family he loved and who loved him. Colorful, realistic illustrations.

Prestine, Joan Singleton. *Someone Special Died.* Los Angeles: Price, Stern, Sloan, Publishers, Inc., 1987.
> Young Rick tells what it feels like to have his best friend die. He is lonely, sad and angry. As he makes a scrapbook of memories, he slowly comes to accept his friend's death. The engaging illustrations and simple text make the story easy for young children to understand.

Sanford, Doris. *It Must Hurt a Lot.* Portland, Oregon: Multnomah Press, 1986.
> A story about the sudden death of Joshua's dog, Muffin, and the lessons Joshua learns about life and death. The lessons are called his "special secrets" and are spelled out in useful ways that can help young children deal with death.

Thurman, Chuck. *A Time for Remembering.* New York: Simon & Schuster, Inc., 1989.
> A boy sits by the fireplace, holding the faded yellow flower that his grandfather gave him before his death. The voices in the next room make the boy feel warm in a different way from the fire. The boy fondly remembers his grandfather, places the flower in the fire and joins his family and friends.

Varley, Susan. *Badger's Parting Gifts.* New York: Lothrop, Lee & Shepard, 1984.
> Badger was a friend, and almost everyone who knew him had warm and loving memories of when he was living with them. At first, those who loved Badger were overwhelmed by his death. In time, though, whenever Badger's name was mentioned, someone would recall something about him that made everyone smile. Badger was part of their lives once more.

Viorst, Judith. *The Tenth Good Thing About Barney.* New York: Atheneum, 1972.
> When Barney the cat dies, his young owner tries to think of ten good things to say at the funeral, but he can only think of nine. As he helps his father in the garden, he realizes that Barney will now help the flowers grow—the tenth good thing. A warm and honest book.

GA1317

Books for Children Ages 8 to 14

Blume, Judy. *Tiger Eyes.* New York: Dell Publishing Company, Inc., 1981.

Davey can't believe that her father has been shot to death in a holdup at his 7-Eleven store. With her mother near collapse and her brother, Jason, too young to understand, Davey and the family move to New Mexico to stay with relatives and try to recover from the shock. Davey discovers a private place in the depths of the Los Alamos Canyon where she begins to put the pieces of her life back together.

Forrai, Marie, and Anders. *Rebecca, A Look at Death.* Minneapolis: Lerner Publications Company, 1978.

The book is a description of the concepts of death through words and photographs. It relates the importance of grief and the customs of mourning.

Hyde, Margaret D., and Lawrence E. Hyde. *Meeting Death.* New York: Walker & Co., 1989.

A straightforward presentation of death-related facts and concepts. Provides information to promote the acceptance of the concept of death, discussing such aspects as the terminally ill, suicide, grief and mourning, and the treatment of death in various cultures. Includes a chapter on helping children deal with a parent's death.

Jury, Mark, and Dan Jury. *Gramp.* New York: Viking, 1976.

A photo history of the life of Frank Tugend and of his death at age 81. Follows him through the good old days, then into his three years of deteriorating mental and physical health, and then his death. It is a realistic look at Frank's failing health and death, as photographed and narrated by those who loved him.

Lee, Virginia. *The Magic Moth.* Seaburg Press, 1972.

This is a story about Mark-O, age 6, and his family, who comes to understand the illness and eventual death of his ten-year-old sister, Maryanne. As Maryanne gets weaker and weaker from heart disease, the father explains to the older children that she is going to die. They work through their feelings as a family and are present when Maryanne dies at home.

Le Shan, Eda. *Learning to Say Good-Bye.* New York: Macmillan Publishing Company, 1976.

The author discusses the questions, fears and fantasies children may have about the parent who has died. The different stages of mourning are discussed. You learn not just about death and grieving, but about life itself.

Mann, Peggy. *There Are Two Kinds of Terrible.* New York: Doubleday & Company, Inc., 1977.

A very readable story for adolescents. It is a moving story of how a young boy faces the death of his beloved mother and must now learn to relate to his withdrawn and sorrowful father.

Mellonie, Bryan, and Robert Ingpen. *Lifetimes: A Beautiful Way to Explain Death to Children.* New York: Bantam Books, 1983.

A moving book for children of all ages. It lets us explain life and death in a sensitive, caring way. It tells about beginnings, endings and living in between. With large, wonderful illustrations, it tells about plants, animals and people. It tells that dying is as much a part of living as being born. It explains how all living things have their own *Lifetimes.*

Norris, Louanne. *An Oak Tree Dies and a Journey Begins.* New York: Crown Publishers, Inc., 1979.

> A scientific account of the ways in which a tree, even after it dies, continues to be an important part of our environment.

Smith, Doris B. *A Taste of Blackberries.* Thomas Y. Crowell, 1973.

> Jamie fooled around a lot, so when he rolled on the ground after a bee sting, his friend thought he was joking. But Jamie died and the friend felt guilty and responsible. The age-old question of "why" is answered by a neighbor who says, "One of the hardest things we have to learn is that some questions do not have answers."

Vogel, Ilse-Margaret. *My Twin Sister Erika.* New York: Harper & Row, 1976.

> A story for elementary-aged children but poignant to all in the sorrowful loss and slow adjustment to the death of a twin sister. Appropriate to any brother and sister loss.

White, E. B. *Charlotte's Web.* Harper & Row, 1952.

> This is an animal fantasy about friendship between Charlotte, a spider, Templeton, a rat, and Wilbur, a pig. When Charlotte dies at the fairgrounds, her friends manage to take her eggs to the farm where they can safely hatch.

Books for Teenagers and Adults

Bluebond-Langner, Myra. *The Private Worlds of Dying Children.* Princeton, New Jersey: Princeton University Press, 1978.

> The author shares her experiences with leukemic children. She explains how children know they are going to die and how they adapt to the death-denying society in which they live out their courageous journey to death.

Bombeck, Erma. *I Want to Grow Hair, I Want to Grow Up, I Want to Go to Boise.* New York: Harper & Row, 1989.

> A heartwarming account of kids surviving cancer. America's favorite family writer brings us the stories of children who have every hope of beating the odds and living to drive their parents crazy. The reader will smile at their wisdom, be dazzled by their insights and share the joys of their triumphs. It is not a medical book, nor is it a sad book. It sparkles with innocence and glistens with hope.

Conley, Herbert N. *Living and Dying Gracefully.* New York: Paulist Press, 1979.

> Reflections of the author's own impending death and how these meditations helped him to live a richer, fuller life.

Fulton, Robert. *Death and Dying: Challenge and Change.* Reading, Massachusetts: Addison-Wesley, 1978.

> Deals with intricate issues of death and dying as found in articles from newspapers and books. Provides a comprehensive overview of death as encountered in modern-day society.

Grollman, Earl. *Concerning Death: A Practical Guide for the Living.* Boston: Beacon Press, 1974.

> Deals with the facts and emotions of death. A practical guide in planning funeral services and making wills.

_____. *Explaining Death to Children.* Boston: Beacon Press, 1967.

> Provides information and practical guides for parents to communicate with their children and help them understand death.

GA1317

_____. *Talking About Death: A Dialogue Between Parent and Child.* Boston: Beacon Press, 1970.

> A sensitive approach toward helping parents deal with a difficult subject. Perceptive and tender as a lyric poem, the author gently guides the reader in coming to terms with death—one of life's processes.

_____. *What Helped Me When My Loved One Died.* Boston: Beacon Press, 1981.

> Offers loving support to those who, having lost a loved one, feel totally alone. It defines the pain of loss and offers constructive ways of coping with the separation of a loved one.

Hamilton, Michael, and Helen Reid. *A Hospice Handbook: A New Way to Care for the Dying.* Grand Rapids: Wm. Eerdman, 1980.

> A succinct and valuable guide to a greater understanding and appreciation of the hospice movement.

James, John W., and Frank Cherry. *The Grief Recovery Handbook.* New York: Harper & Row, 1988.

> A novel approach to the resolution of grief as practiced by the authors in their roles as grief counselors. In partnership with one or more other grievers, one reviews past losses and the ways in which those losses were resolved. Honesty and free expression of emotions, no matter how long they have been smothered, are the keys.

Kastenbaum, Robert. *Psychology of Death.* New York: Springer, 1972.

> An excellent resource for every library. Gives a comprehensive review of various aspects of death.

Kavanaugh, Robert. *Facing Death.* New York: Penguin, 1974.

> A compelling book that forces the reader to examine his attitudes about death. Discusses such issues as euthanasia, suicide and the value and purpose of funerals.

Kubler-Ross, Elisabeth. *Living with Death and Dying.* New York: Macmillan Publishing Company, 1981.

> An insightful book that causes the reader to take a serious look at the Gospel message regarding the sick and the dead. The author's work spans a decade of caring for the terminally ill, including the total needs unique to the dying.

_____. *Questions and Answers on Death and Dying.* New York: Macmillan Publishing Company, 1974.

> A selection of the author's most frequently asked questions and candid answers about dying. It's a sequel to *On Death and Dying* and covers such topics as the dying person, suicide, funerals and problems encountered by the family of the dying person.

Schweidman, Edwin. *Death: Current Perspectives.* Palo Alto, California: Mayfield Press, 1976.

> A compilation of changing trends in thanatology. Provides a broad summary of contemporary insights about death and dying.

Smith, Kathleen. *The Stress of Sorrow.* Dallas, Texas: Southwest Book Services, 1978.

> Treats death as a process of life. Graphically describes all phases of sorrow including, in a sensitive way, the unique grief and sorrow associated with suicide, murder, abortion.

GA1317

Service Organizations for Death Education

Candlelighters Childhood Cancer Foundation
1312 18th Street N.W., Suite 200
Washington, D.C. 20036
(202) 659-5136
An international organization for parents of children with cancer.

The Center for Attitudinal Healing
19 Main Street
Tiburon, CA 94920
(415) 435-5022
A family center that also supports group meetings of children who have to face life and death situations because of their illnesses.

Children's Hospice International
1101 King Street, Suite 131
Alexandria, VA 22314
(703) 684-0330
An international organization that encourages hospice care of terminally ill children as an alternative to the traditional institutional system.

Compassionate Friends
P.O. Box 3696
Oak Brook, IL 60522
(708) 990-0010
National organization offering emotional and educational support to families with children who have died.

The Elisabeth Kubler-Ross Center
Headwater, VA 24442
(703) 396-3441
A nonprofit, nonsectarian organization dedicated to the enhancement of life and growth through the practice of unconditional love.

Make a Wish Foundation
1624 E. Meadowbrook
Phoenix, AZ 85016
(602) 248-9474 (WISH)
Fulfills favorite wish of any child under eighteen who has a life-threatening illness.

Parents of Murdered Children
100 E. 8th Street, B-41
Cincinnati, OH 45237
(513) 721-5683
An ongoing support group for families who have lost a child, parent or spouse by murder.

Pen Pals for Terminally Ill Teenagers
Teenagers can write:
"Pen Pal," KCAL TV
5515 Melrose Avenue
Los Angeles, CA 90038

GA1317